Cultural Traditions in

Turkey

Joan Marie Galat

Crabtree Publishing Company
www.crabtreebooks.com

Crabtree Publishing Company
www.crabtreebooks.com

For Cousin Richard, with love

Author: Joan Marie Galat

Publishing plan research and development:
Reagan Miller

Editorial director: Kathy Middleton

Editor: Ellen Rodger

Proofreader: Wendy Scavuzzo

Photo research: Abigail Smith

Designer: Abigail Smith

Production coordinator and prepress technician:
Abigail Smith

Print coordinator: Margaret Amy Salter

Cover: Turkish patterns (top, bkgd); Wall frescoes that decorate the Elmali Kilise or Apple Church in Cappadocia, Turkey (middle); traditional Turkish coffee and Turkish delight (middle right); pomegranate fruit (bottom bkgd); tarboosh hat (bottom middle); saz baglama instrument (bottom right); Sufi dancer (middle)

Title page: Turkish folk dancers.

Photographs:
Getty Images: Anadolu Agency, p13 (left); MUSTAFA OZER, p18
Shutterstock: © Faraways, front cover (center); © natalia_maroz, front cover (middle bkgd); © akturer, title page; © thomas koch, p9 (inset); © fulya atalay, pp12, 15 (bottom); © dnd_project, p14; © oykuozgu, p15 (top); © muratart, pp16, 17 (bottom); © EvrenKalinbacak, p17 (top); © muratart, pp19, 29 (top); © ymphotos, p22 (right); © M DOGAN, p23; © Yavuz Sariyildiz, p24; © arda savasciogullari, pp26-27 (bottom); © deepspace, p28; © Orlok, p29 (bottom); © Dreamer Company, p30 (bottom)
Wikimedia Commons: Yok, p11 (top right); ozgurmulazimoglu, p11 (bottom); Celal Bayar University, p18; MoserB, p22 (left); Lapost, p31 (inset)

All other images by Shutterstock

Library and Archives Canada Cataloguing in Publication

Galat, Joan Marie, 1963-, author
    Cultural traditions in Turkey / Joan Marie Galat.

(Cultural traditions in my world)
Includes index.
Issued in print and electronic formats.
ISBN 978-0-7787-8100-4 (hardcover).--
ISBN 978-0-7787-8108-0 (softcover).--
ISBN 978-1-4271-1955-1 (HTML)

    1. Holidays--Turkey--Juvenile literature. 2. Festivals--Turkey--Juvenile literature. 3. Turkey--Social life and customs--Juvenile literature. I. Title. II. Series: Cultural traditions in my world

GT4873.5.A2G35 2017   j394.269561   C2017-903532-0
                                       C2017-903533-9

Library of Congress Cataloging-in-Publication Data

Names: Galat, Joan Marie, 1963- author.
Title: Cultural traditions in Turkey / Joan Marie Galat.
Description: New York, New York : Crabtree Publishing, 2018. |
    Series: Cultural traditions in my world | Includes index. |
    Audience: Age 5-8. | Audience: Grad K to 3.
Identifiers: LCCN 2017024409 (print) | LCCN 2017027892 (ebook) |
    ISBN 9781427119551 (Electronic HTML) |
    ISBN 9780778781004 (reinforced library binding) |
    ISBN 9780778781080 (pbk.)
Subjects: LCSH: Festivals--Turkey--Juvenile literature. | Turkey--Social life and customs--Juvenile literature.Classification: LCC GT4873.5.A2 (ebook) |
    LCC GT4873.5.A2 G35 2018 (print) | DDC 394.269561--dc23
LC record available at https://lccn.loc.gov/2017024409

Crabtree Publishing Company
www.crabtreebooks.com   1-800-387-7650

Printed in Canada/082017/EF20170629

Published in Canada
Crabtree Publishing
616 Welland Ave.
St. Catharines, ON
L2M 5V6

Published in the United States
Crabtree Publishing
PMB 59051
350 Fifth Avenue, 59th Floor
New York, New York 10118

Published in the United Kingdom
Crabtree Publishing
Maritime House
Basin Road North, Hove
BN41 1WR

Published in Australia
Crabtree Publishing
3 Charles Street
Coburg North
VIC 3058

Contents

Welcome to Turkey

Turkey is a country that is located on two continents: Asia and Europe. More than 80 million people live in the nation's 81 provinces. Most are Turkish, with **Kurds** being the largest of more than 20 **ethnic** groups. The official language is Turkish, but Kurdish and other languages are also spoken.

Did You Know?
Ninety-seven percent of Turkey is located in Asia.

BULGARIA

Black Sea

Europe

Asia

GEORGIA

TURKEY

GREECE

CYPRUS

IRAQ

SYRIA

Mediterranean Sea

LEBANON

Almost all Turks are **Sunni Muslims**. Their religious holidays follow a lunar calendar based on the Moon's phases. This makes holidays occur earlier each year. National holidays in Turkey fall on the same date each year. They follow the Gregorian calendar, based on Earth's travel around the Sun.

Did You Know?
Each region, or area, in Turkey has its own festivals. Some celebrate sports, such as camel wrestling. Others, such as the cherry and apricot festivals, celebrate harvest time.

Special Days

A new baby is a happy event for the entire community. Anatolia is the Asian part of Turkey. There, mothers and new babies may stay inside for 40 days, to protect the baby from harm. Baby naming includes a celebration and blessing. Everyone prays, then a religious leader or the father whispers the name into the child's ear three times.

Did You Know?
In Anatolia, it is common to celebrate the first time a child's nails are trimmed. After the nails are cut, the baby's hands are placed into a bag of money. The money the child grabs is saved for the child's future.

Engagements are celebrated with a party. An older relative gives the couple rings. They wear them on their right hands before marrying, and on the left after. Traditional three-day weddings include coloring the bride's hands and feet with henna, planting a wedding flag, and a parade to fetch the bride.

Henna is a reddish-brown dye used to create beautiful patterns on skin.

New Year

As in many other parts of the world, it is a Turkish tradition to begin celebrating the upcoming year on New Year's Day, January 1. In bigger cities, houses may be decorated. Family and friends often exchange cards and presents. A lottery ticket is a common gift, because a major national lottery is held at that time. Turks enjoy a big family dinner, play games, or watch fireworks, such as the ones below in Istanbul.

Some people smash pomegranates on the floor so the seeds, which represent good luck, will spill out.

In Anatolia, Nevruz is held on March 21–22 to celebrate the New Year according to the lunar calendar. Nevruz can represent a new farming season, a religious event, or a time to remember the dead.

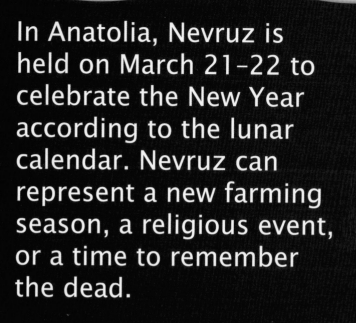

Did You Know?
The Kurds celebrate Nevruz with a bonfire on March 21 or 22. Nevruz means "new day" in Kurdish.

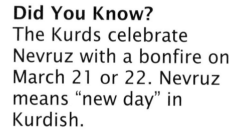

National Sovereignty and Children's Day

National **Sovereignty** and Children's Day celebrates the anniversary of Turkey's first parliament, called the Grand National Assembly, on April 23, 1920. A parliament is a group of people who make laws. This holiday also celebrates the importance of children. It is tradition for children to take the place of the president, prime minister, and other top government leaders at the Grand National Assembly.

Children meet at parliament to discuss things such as children's issues, education, and the environment.

Other special events include recitals, dances, and activities that allow people to celebrate together. Children also wear new clothes on this day, and go door-to-door collecting candy.

Did You Know?
Turkey's first president, Mustafa Kemal Atatürk, dedicated April 23 to Turkey's children. To honor him, people hang out flags and put up pictures of Atatürk.

Children may perform songs for a crowd to honor the holiday.

Kirkpinar Festival

The Kirkpinar Festival is one of the oldest festivals in Turkey. It is held in the city of Edirne in July. The event is a series of matches between wrestlers called *pehlivans*. They play a unique game called *yagli gures*, which means "oiled wrestling." Players cover their bodies in olive oil and wear pants made of leather from cattle or water buffalo, called *kisbet* or *kispet*.

More than 1,000 boys and men compete in the festival.

As the pehlivans wrestle, bands play Turkish instruments such as *davul* drums and *zurna*, shown here atop the drum.

The event begins with a ceremony that includes music. The Kirkpinar Golden Belt, shown above, is carried in a parade, and each pehlivan's name is announced. The winner receives the golden belt, and is named Chief Pehlivan.

Labor and Solidarity Day

Labor and Solidarity Day, also called May Day, is a tradition that is more than 100 years old. It is an official holiday. Some people use the day to ask for better pay and fair treatment for workers and women. Marches and **demonstrations** are held across the country. Concerts and ceremonies also take place. Many gather at Istanbul's Taksim Square. While huge crowds demonstrate, others simply enjoy time off work. May Day can be one of the first warm days of spring.

Some people lay wreaths at the **Republic** Monument in Taksim Square.

Many Turks wear red clothing on May Day.

Did You Know?
People often greet one another by saying "Yaşasın 1 Mayıs", which means "Long live 1st of May."

Commemoration of Atatürk

After **World War I**, Greek forces invaded Turkey. Atatürk traveled to the city of Samsun to organize a revolution. He arrived on May 19, 1919. This was the start of Turkey's move toward independence, or ruling itself. It is remembered with a national holiday on May 19, called the **Commemoration** of Atatürk.

Turkish folk dances are performed at all celebrations.

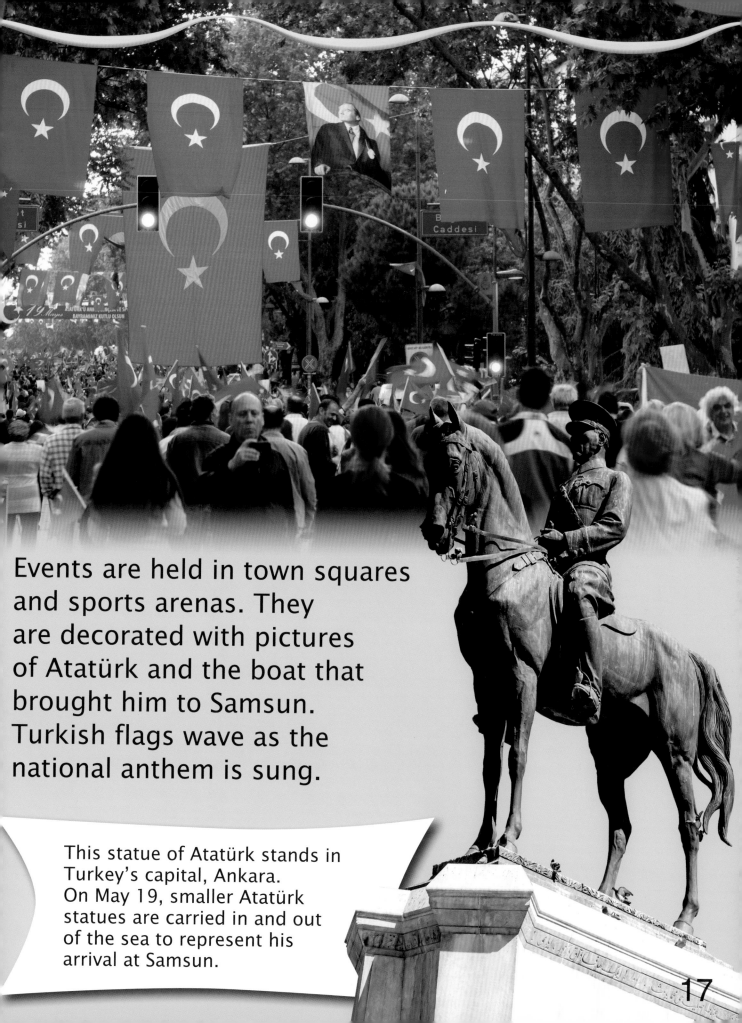

Events are held in town squares and sports arenas. They are decorated with pictures of Atatürk and the boat that brought him to Samsun. Turkish flags wave as the national anthem is sung.

This statue of Atatürk stands in Turkey's capital, Ankara. On May 19, smaller Atatürk statues are carried in and out of the sea to represent his arrival at Samsun.

Youth and Sports Day

Atatürk felt that youth were important to Turkey's future. He created Youth and Sports Day to encourage young people and promote physical activity. On May 19, parades bring the streets to life. Marching bands, sporting events, and flag-carrying ceremonies add to the festivities.

Turkish students perform for a crowd on Youth and Sports Day by building a human tower.

Youth may participate in marches, shown below, and listen to speeches. Athletes carry the Turkish flag to the Samsun Harbor shore. Youth carry a Turkish flag and soil from Samsun to Ankara, to be presented to Turkey's president at a special ceremony. This national holiday is also a popular time to visit Atatürk's **mausoleum** in Ankara, known as Anıtkabir.

Ramadan

Ramadan is the holiest month for Muslims. Every year for the ninth month of the Islamic lunar calendar, Muslims **fast** between sunrise and sunset. The fast ends with prayer, followed by a meal that can last late into the night. The end of Ramadan is celebrated with a feast of traditional foods, such as a spinach and cheese pastry called *borek*.

Dessert may include sweet, syrupy *kunefe,* made of cheese, sugar, and crushed pistachios on top.

Şeker Bayramı, the Turkish name for Eid al-Fitr, is a three-day national holiday that follows Ramadan. The mood on the streets is cheerful. Vendors sell food and fireworks light the sky. Children may receive toys, clothing, and other gifts. Younger family members visit older relatives and guests are given candies.

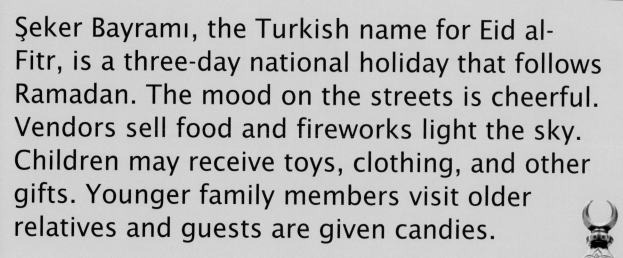

On religious holidays, it is tradition for a young person to kiss the hands of their parents and older relatives. The kiss shows love and respect.

Did You Know?
Şeker Bayramı is also called the Sugar Festival. Sweets such as *rahat lokum*, or Turkish delight (above), are served after a meal.

Victory Day

After World War I, European armies took over Istanbul. Turkey fought the War of Independence to remove them. It won a final fight on August 30, 1922. On the anniversary, Victory Day is celebrated to remember those who died in the battle.

Did You Know?
Meals, rituals, and ceremonies are held when soldiers begin and end military service. One tradition is for relatives to give new soldiers money for good luck.

The Turkish Air Force performs a show on Victory Day.

This national holiday, also called Army Day, is a lively event. It is celebrated with parades, military band concerts, and speeches about freedom. Turkish flags and pictures of Atatürk decorate buildings. Wreaths are laid at Atatürk's mausoleum. Around the country, people gather at statues of Atatürk to watch Victory Day ceremonies.

Members of the Turkish military proudly march and wave flags at this parade in Ankara.

Feast of the Sacrifice

The Feast of the **Sacrifice** is celebrated to remember the story of Abraham. In that story, the Muslim god Allah asks Abraham to sacrifice his son Ibrahim to prove his faith. When Allah saw Abraham about to obey, he allowed him to kill a ram as a sacrifice instead of Ibrahim.

Cattle markets are created in the streets for the event.

During this four-day national holiday, sheep are led through the streets and people may buy an animal to sacrifice. The family keeps one third of the meat and gives the rest to family and friends, or people in need. It is a time to feast on traditional foods that might include kebabs, stuffed vine leaves, and *bumbar dolmasi*—grilled intestines stuffed with liver.

Vine leaves are usually stuffed with rice, spices, and vegetables.

Kebabs are made with roasted meat.

Republic Day

Republic Day celebrates the anniversary of the beginning of the Turkish Republic. On October 29, 1923, Turkey became an independent country. Ankara became the capital, and war hero Mustafa Kemal Atatürk became the country's first president. The national holiday is October 29, but celebrations often begin the night before.

Did You Know?
Mustafa Kemal changed his last name to Atatürk, which means father of the Turks. No one else in Turkey is allowed to be called Atatürk.

Turks decorate the streets with the nation's flag. They may attend a speech, military parade, or ceremony to honor Atatürk and the republic. Many people visit Atatürk's mausoleum. Musicians play the national anthem. Events such as a public concert or an air show, in which pilots demonstrate their flying skills, add to the celebration.

Fireworks end the Republic Day celebrations.

Death of Atatürk

The anniversary of Mustafa Kemal Atatürk's death is not an official holiday, but the day is remembered across the country. At 9:05 a.m. on November 10, Turks stop what they are doing and are silent for one minute. Fire alarms and police sirens are sounded at the moment when Atatürk died in 1938.

These Turks in Istanbul stop their cars to be silent at 9:05 a.m.

Wreaths are laid at Atatürk statues, flags are flown at half-mast, and school children take part in activities to honor the country's founder. The biggest event is at his mausoleum. Every year, tens of thousands of people gather there to remember Atatürk.

All over the country, ceremonies take place to honor Atatürk.

Mevlana Festival

The Mevlana Festival is Turkey's largest festival. It honors the death of Mevlana Celaleddin Rumi—a poet and thinker who encouraged peace. Rumi's son founded the Mevlevi Order, a religious group. On December 17, the anniversary of Rumi's death, people from across Turkey, and the world, go to the city of Konya to honor Rumi. They attend readings, concerts, and the seven-part *sema* ceremony.

Mevlevi members, known as whirling *dervishes*, perform a dance on December 17. Their white robes flare outward as they spin around up to 30 times a minute.

The Feast of Saint Nicholas celebrates the man known as Santa Claus, or in Turkish as Noel Baba. It is celebrated in Turkey in the first week of December. People remember his kindness and generosity.

This building in Konya is the place where Rumi is buried. It is also a museum that holds objects that are important to the Mevlevi Order.

Glossary

Allah The name of God in Islam

commemoration A call to remember something important

demonstrations Events where people come together to show how they feel about something

ethnic Relating to a group with a common background or culture

fast To not eat food for a period of time

Kurds An ethnic group who live in southeastern Turkey

mausoleum A stone building where the body of an important person is laid to rest

republic A country or state in which citizens vote for their leaders

sacrifice To offer something precious to Allah, such as the life of an animal

sovereignty The right of a country to be and rule itself

Sunni Muslims The largest branch of Muslims, who follow the religion Islam

World War I A major war between the Allied Nations (Great Britain and Canada, Australia, France, Russia, the United States) and the Central Powers (Germany, Austro-Hungary, Turkey)

Index